ĀDI ŚAṄKARĀCĀRYA'S

Shiva Manas Puja

Worship Within

Commentary by
Swami Tejomayananda

Central Chinmaya Mission Trust

Printed from Feb. 2006 to Mar. 2009 - 3000 copies
Revised Edition - November 2010 - 2000 copies
Third Edition - January 2014 - 2000 copies
Reprint - December 2017 - 1500 copies
Reprint - May 2025 - 1000 copies

Published by:
Chinmaya Prakashan
The Publications Division of
Central Chinmaya Mission Trust
Sandeepany Sadhanalaya
Saki Vihar Road, Powai, Mumbai - 400072, India
Tel.: +91-22-2803 4900
Email: ccmtpublications@chinmayamission.com
Website: www.chinmayamission.com

Distribution Centre in the USA:
Chinmaya Publications West
560 Bridgetown Pike
Feasterville, PA 19053-7240, USA
Tel.: (215) 396-0390, Fax: (215) 396-9710
Email: publications@chinmayamission.org
Website: www.chinmayapublications.com

Cover Designed by: Mayapuri Graphics, Chennai

Printed by: SAP Print Solutions Pvt. Ltd., Mumbai

ISBN: 978-81-7597-500-2

Publisher's Note

Everything about the Lord is 'Satyam Śivam Sundaram' (Truth-Auspiciousness-Beauty) – His names, forms, qualities, nature... He is, therefore, truly worshipful (pūjya), as are His worshippers (pūjakas).

Parama Pūjya Guruji Swami Tejomayananda, gave discourses on the *Śiva Mānasa Pūjā* (the mental worship of Lord Śiva) of Ādi Śaṅkarācārya in February 2005 as his worship (pūjā) of the Lord on the occasion of the inauguration of a Śiva Temple. We are glad to present these words of worship in a book form as our offering at the feet of the Lord.

Further, wherever footnotes are given in Sanskrit Devanāgarī scripts, their English transliterations are given at the end of this book to facilitate the readers.

It was His grace that makes all efforts possible. May His grace be ever on all His worshippers.

Central Chinmaya Mission Trust
Mumbai - 400 072

Transliteration and Pronunciation Guide

In the book, Devanāgarī characters are transliterated according to the scheme adopted by the International Congress of Orientalists at Athens in 1912. In it one fixed pronunciation value is given to each letter; f, q, w, x and z are not called to use. According to this scheme:

Devanāgarī	Translit-eration	Sounds Like	Devanāgarī	Translit-eration	Sounds Like
अ	a	son	ढ्	ḍh	adhesive*
आ	ā	father	ण्	ṇ	under*
इ	i	different	त्	t	tabla
ई	ī	feel	थ्	th	thumb
उ	u	full	द्	d	this
ऊ	ū	boot	ध्	dh	Gandhi
ऋ	ṛ	rhythm*	न्	n	nose
ॠ	ṝ	**	प्	p	pen
ऌ	ḷ	**	फ्	ph	phantom*
ए	e	evade	ब्	b	boil
ऐ	ai	delight	भ्	bh	abhor
ओ	o	core	म्	m	mind
औ	au	now	य्	y	yes
क्	k	calm	र्	r	right
ख्	kh	khan	ल्	l	love
ग्	g	gate	व्	v	very
घ्	gh	ghost	श्	ś	shut
ङ्	ṅ	ankle*	ष	ṣ	sugar
च्	c	chuckle	स्	s	simple
छ्	ch	witch*	ह्	h	happy
ज्	j	justice	ं	ṁ	improvise
झ्	jh	Jhansi	ः	ḥ	**
ञ्	ñ	banyan	क्ष्	kṣ	action
ट्	ṭ	tank	त्र्	tr	three*
ठ्	ṭh	**	ज्ञ्	jñ	gnosis
ड्	ḍ	dog	ऽ	'	a silent 'a'

* These letters do not have an exact English equivalent. An approximation is given here.

** These sounds cannot be approximated in English words.

Introduction

The Śiva (Śiva's) Mānasa (mental) Pūjā (worship) is a prayer (stotra) in praise of God written by Ādi Śaṅkarācārya. Worship involves the act of worship (pūjā) done with a worshipful attitude (pūjya bhāva). A mere mechanical act without the exalted feeling and right attitude is joyless and meaningless. Also feelings unexpressed in words or actions too, give no results. Feelings find fulfilment, when expressed in action. We find that often love expresses in serving the beloved. When there are feelings, there is a greater chance of them culminating in action. However, mechanical action too, when done over a period of time, have a better chance of kindling or intensifying feelings than no action at all. We see that worship done as routine, in time, creates the worshipful attitude and devotion in the heart of the worshipper. Hence, the act of worship too has its own place of importance.

In worship, there exists the triad of the worshipper (pūjaka), the altar of worship (pūjya) and the act of worship (pūjā). Let us now explore and think about them.

Pūjya – Who is the altar of worship? All of us, even those who do not believe in God, have ideals. We idolize a person, who exemplifies our ideals or a cause that personifies them. We may not use words like worship, but we do value, respect and idolize someone or the other. Such feelings do find expression in various ways.

So, whom do we respect, worship or idolize? This depends largely on what we value. We respect a person, who exemplifies, or, at least to some extent has, what we value. Some give importance to age, and so respect elders. Others value wealth, power, health, knowledge, character, talent, nature and so on, and, therefore, respect the rich, powerful, healthy, knowledgeable, virtuous, talented and natural beauty respectively. The more we find the characteristics we value in an individual, the more we respect him/her. (The lack of these in some, may also cause disrespect). Imagine one who has all the characteristics we value and give importance to, and that too, in infinite measure. Would we not have the highest respect for him/her? Would he/she not become the most worshipful?

Īśvara – The Lord is Himself infinite, and has infinite virtues. (Rāma – ananta, ananta guṇa). The existence of the part itself proves the existence of the infinite (ananta). The water in all the taps proves the existence of water in the overhead tank. God is the infinite treasure house of all virtues. An individual's virtues may be acquired, cultivated, inherited, earned or given up. They increase, decrease and sometimes disappear altogether. However, the virtues of the Lord are inherent. They are His very nature, inseparable from Him (abhinna) and hence, ever present in Him.

The Truth (God) is one, but is spoken of by the wise in many ways.[1] He is one, His names and forms are many. One of His names is Śiva – the auspicious one. As the Lord, He is the creator, sustainer and destroyer of the world. People generally call Lord Śiva, the destroyer of the universe. However, the three functions go on simultaneously in creation. Once the mother scolded the child, "Why did you

---

[1] एकं सद्विप्रा बहुधा वदन्ति – ऋग्वेद–१·१६४·४६

break the glass?" The child replied "Look at it this way. I've created many glass pieces!" Śiva is the one who blesses (anugraha) and controls (nigraha) all beings. He is Rudra – the terrible, who terrifies the evil. Rudra is one, who makes others weep.[1] The evil cry, when they are punished, and the devoted cry, when their hearts are filled with love for the Lord. Śiva is the formless Truth (Brahman), who alone assumes all the forms of the world. He is the omniscient, omnipotent Lord.[2] He presides over all actions and makes sure, that their results reach people in accordance with the law of karma.[3] He symbolizes faith.[4] He is both, an ideal devotee (of Śrī Rāma) and the altar of devotion. He is seen both, as a meditator and the one meditated upon. He is easily pleased (āśutoṣa). He fulfils our desires and destroys them as well. Being the very source of all knowledge, He is also the first Teacher – Ādi-guru. – 'I bow down to Śiva, who is the eternal Knowledge incarnate Guru.'[5] He is the initiator of

---

1 रोदयति इति (*rodayati iti*)

2 सर्वज्ञ सर्वशक्तिमान् (*sarvajña sarvaśaktimān*)

3 कर्माध्यक्ष कर्मफलदाता (*karmādhyakṣa karmaphaladātā*)

4 भवानी शंकरौ वन्दे श्रद्धा विश्वास रूपिणौ – तुलसी रामायण–१·२

5 वन्दे बोधमयं नित्यं गुरुं शंकर रूपिणम् – तुलसी रामायण–१·३

the teacher-taught lineage (Guru-śiṣya paramparā) through which all knowledge, especially spiritual knowledge, is transmitted from beginningless time till now. We are the blessed recipients of this same knowledge.

'I prostrate to the teacher-taught lineage, which starts from Śiva, continues till Śaṅkarācārya, and further up to my own Guru.'[1]

In *Śiva Mahimna Stotra*, Śrī Puṣpadanta writes, 'Even if Sarasvatī – the Goddess of knowledge – Herself were to write forever, she would not be able to describe the endless virtues, glories and characteristics of the Lord.'[2]

Pūjaka – Who is the worshipper and why does he worship? The individual, who well appreciates his limitations (alpatvam), and looks upon the infinite nature of the Lord, is naturally filled with awe and respect. He cannot help, but worship the infinite

---

1 सदाशिव समारम्भां शंकराचार्य मध्यमाम्।
अस्मदाचार्य पर्यन्तां वन्दे गुरु परम्पराम्॥

2 लिखति यदि गृहीत्वा शारदा सर्वकालं तदपि तव गुणानां ईश पारं न याति
– शिव महिम्न स्तोत्र – ३२

Lord, when he realizes that, all that he has, is given by Him, and that, he is a part of the Lord. We profusely thank a person, if he/she were to gift us rings, earrings and bangles. Then should we not thank the one, who gave us the fingers, ears and hands to wear them? One can buy jewellery, but can one buy one's limbs? Can artificial limbs be as precious as the real ones? When we realize the abundance with which the Lord gives, we feel deeply indebted and grateful to the Lord, and so worship Him.

When we feel hopeless and helpless, we seek refuge in the one, who is all-capable. To whom else can we surrender but the Lord? When we trip and fall, we take the support of the very ground, on which we fall, to get up. Do we stop drinking water, just because the tsunami waters destroyed so many? Do we not rebuild our homes and cities on the very same earth, which destroyed them by its tremors? The Lord alone is the refuge for the needy and helpless. One who realizes that, respects and worships Him.

Many worship God, as He fulfils our desires. Some may question, 'Is it right to ask the Lord for anything? Would that not be selfish? Should we not worship Him for His own sake?' True, that would be the best. But, we do have desires, and the Lord is capable of fulfilling them. So, if we wish to ask, it is better to ask Him than beg before the world. We should ask Him, but not keep on asking Him. Also once the desire is fulfilled, we should not forget Him. We should not by our ingratitude, actualize the proverb, 'God gives and forgives. Man gets and forgets!' And more important, if the desire is not fulfilled, we should not doubt Him, or get angry with Him. One man said that he lost faith in God, when he did not get the transfer he desired, so, he transferred God from his altar! Our faith is shaken or destroyed, when we think of Him only as a 'wish-fulfiller' and not as a 'well-wisher'. If we realize, that whatever He ordains, is for our best, we would not be disappointed, dejected or plunged into doubt, when our wish is not fulfilled. We should continue to worship and pray to Him. A sick child demands an ice cream, and screams at his parents for not fulfilling his wish, little realizing, what is good for him. Many of our demands are childish and contradictory. To demand that every wish of ours be fulfilled, is illogical. A bowler prays, that he will get the batsman clean bowled, and the batsman simultaneously prays, that he should hit a sixer from that very same ball! It is impossible for both their wishes to be fulfilled. A true devotee prays, 'May I gain devotion for the Lord life after life.[1] A sāttvika person prays, 'May I improve myself.' A mature person knows, 'I will get, what I deserve, and not just what I desire.'

The Lord does not gain anything by our worship. He does not need to be worshipped or ask for the worship. It is we, who stand to gain by worshipping Him. A house does not ask to be cleaned and done up. It is we who feel good entering a clean, well arranged and decorated home. In one home it was written, 'Welcome! You are seeing my home in disorder. It is not always so. Most of the time it is worse!' On our child's first birthday, he does not understand, what is happening – why he is overdressed and smothered with attention? It is we, who get joy and fulfilment in the celebration. Similarly, the worshipper alone benefits by his act of worship and worshipful attitude.

---

[1] जनम जनम रति राम पद यह बरदानु न आन – अयोध्याकाण्ड – २०४

Not to worship one, who is worshipful, is wrong, and to worship one, who does not deserve worship, is also wrong (aparādha). 'Giving up the company of the good, I serve the evil, day and night. There cannot be anyone more crooked than me,' laments Saint Sūradāsa.[1] It is interesting to note, that saintly people like Sūradāsa feel bad about their little weaknesses, while most of us justify even our big flaws!

Thus, the individual worships to express his love, reverence and gratitude out of helplessness, or to fulfil his desires.

Pūjā – How should we worship? Pūjā is done with the body (kāyika), speech (vācika) and the mind (mānasika). With concentration and feeling we chant the mantras and perform the rituals. Hence, all three – body, speech and mind are involved, and in the process, get tuned up. Mental worship (mānasika pūjā), however, is more difficult and subtle, as only the mind is involved, and hence, there is only one support. Riding a tricycle or a bicycle is definitely easier than a monocycle, which requires a lot of practice and special

---

[1] हरिजन छांडि हरी-विमुखन की निसदिन करत गुलामी।
मो सम कौन कुटिल खल कामी॥ – सूरदास

talent. However, there is more freedom in mental worship. There is no limitation of material, money or efforts. We can offer all that we desire, inasmuch quantity as we wish and of the best imaginable quality. In fact, we can offer heavenly offerings, which we may never have personally experienced but only heard about, or create our own unique imagined offerings.

People normally find a hundred excuses for not performing, doing spiritual practices like pūjā, or visiting the temple. 'I am unwell', 'I cannot afford rituals', 'I have no time', 'I do not know the chants', 'there is no place at home where I can worship' and so on. All these do not apply in mental worship. You can do so lying in bed (if you are unable to sit up, and even if you are a pauper), at any time, in any place and in any way, you desire. Of course, since the object of our worship is the Lord Himself, we should try to maintain a respectful posture and a conducive atmosphere, as such physical aspects do have an impact on the mind.

Normally, people feel pūjā is a mechanical action, which has to be 'got over and done with' as part of one's daily routine (dinacaryā).

People say, 'pūjā kar ḍālī' (Hindi), or 'pūjā karī nākhī' (Gujarati), which indicates, that one has finished it with a sense of relief that it is over, rather than with a sense of fulfilment of having done it well. Our attitude should be 'pūjā kar lī' – completed (with good feelings derived from it).

When one matures, one realizes that pūjā (worship) is a continuous process, which happens all through the day, in and through every action of ours. It does not remain a particular act done for a particular period of time.

The ritual of pūjā requires materials, money to buy them, effort, the ritualistic know-how, time, the chanting of various mantras and so on. However, when we perform mental worship, no money or materials are required. The effort is in performing the act mentally. This is possible, only if we have first done the same physically, or at least, witnessed it with keen observation. Of course, we can discover our own way of worship. That too is acceptable to the Lord. However, the traditional techniques and methods are time-tested and are highly effective. So we should try to learn them.

What is the use of staying in close proximity with a great Master and not gaining any of his virtues? Pūjā is a form of upāsanā – a spiritual practice. When we practise regularly, we imbibe the divine virtues of our altar of worship, and ultimately become one with the worshipped.[1] This is the highest result of worship. To directly worship God, when He appears in front of us, is a joy unparalleled and for most of us, an unimaginable occurance. Rare ones, like Śabarī, enjoyed such bliss. For us, however, the ritualistic physical worship is done by invoking the Lord in an idol or a picture. Since our mind is gross, it is easier for us to appreciate the Lord with a form. We must, however, understand that what we worship is not the idol (stone or wood), but the ideal behind the idol. Also, God is not 'only in the idol', but 'also in the idol'. He is all-pervading and His glory is to be seen in all.

The sixteen steps of ritualistic worship – The ritualistic worship of God is done in sixteen steps (ṣoḍaśa upacāra), just as an honoured guest is received and entertained in a traditional Hindu home. We cleanse and decorate our home (pūrva pūjā) and

1 ···मम साधर्म्यमागताः – गीता -१४·२

await the arrival of the guest/God (dhyānam). On arrival, we welcome (āvāhanam) and seat the guest/God (āsanam), wash His/Her feet (pādyam), hands (arghyam) and offer water to drink (ācamanam). Nowadays, we offer tea, coffee or aerated drinks. If a guest has come from afar, he refreshes himself with a bath (snānam), a special bath (abhiṣeka), dons fresh clothes (vastram), grooms himself (alaṅkāram), applies perfume (candanam, akṣata), and is honoured with flowers (puṣpam, arcanam), fragrance (dhūpam), showing lights (dīpam), offering of food (naivedyam), entertainment (rāja upacāra), vesper lights (nīrājanam), the offer of gifts (dakṣiṇā), circumambulation and prostration (pradakṣiṇā, namaskāram) and bidding farewell (visarjanam). Such worship can be done elaborately for hours, or by a brief ceremony in just a few steps. It can be done according to Vaidika, Smārta, Paurāṇika or Tāntrika methods, or a mixture of these. Whatever the method adopted, it is the feeling and attitude behind the worship (bhāva), that is more important.

Now let us see how to do the pūjā – Here, we are talking about mental worship (mānasika pūjā) in particular. The first step is dhyānam/meditation.

Dhyānam, as a step in ritualistic worship, involves reverential visualization of the form of the Lord we love the most.[1] It is to be noted that the Lord is one, but can assume many or any form. Such focused visualization and contemplation and its significance, fills us with devotion and longing for the worship that follows. The worship then becomes 'love made visible'.

Fortunately for us, the compassionate Lord assumes whichever form we love.[2] 'The Lord fortifies our faith in whichever form, we desire to worship Him'.[3]

If the Lord could assume only one form, how could He be called omnipotent? Also, all of us have different natures and propensities. It would be impossible to decide on form, which is universally loved.

Pūjya Gurudev Swami Chinmayananda used to present this point with an amusing, yet powerful

---

1 इष्ट रूप ध्यानम् (*iṣṭa rūpa dhyānam.*)

2 ये यथा मां प्रपद्यन्ते तांस्तथैव भजाम्यहम्। – गीता-४·११

3 यो यो यां यां तनुं भक्तः श्रद्धयार्चितुमिच्छति।
तस्य तस्याचलां श्रद्धां तामेव विदधाम्यहम्॥ – गीता-७·२१

example. When we invite friends over for dinner, don't we serve several dishes to suit the varying palates of the guests? Supposing, we placed one fat pot of curd rice on the centre of the table, and expected all to eat it, would it be a successful dinner party?

Please note again that, Hindu dharma does not believe in many gods and goddesses. There is one God alone. However, the Lord assumes varied forms to inspire our varied minds.

Saint Tulasīdāsa meditates on Lord Śiva thus –

Lord Śiva is one, on whose side shines (resides) Pārvatī, who carries the celestial Ganga on His head, on whose brow rests the crescent moon, whose throat holds poison, and whose chest is adorned with a huge serpent, and His body with ashes, who is great amongst the deities, the Lord of all, the destroyer of the universe, the omnipresent Śiva, who, like the moon is pleasant and auspicious. May He, ever protect me.[1]

---

1 यस्याङ्के च विभाति भूधरसुता देवापगा मस्तके
भाले बालविधुर्गले च गरलं यस्योरसि व्यालराट्।
सोऽयं भूतिविभूषणः सुरवरः सर्वाधिपः सर्वदा
शर्वः सर्वगतः शिवः शशिनिभः श्रीशङ्करः पातु माम्॥ – अयोध्या-काण्ड – मंगलाचरण

Śiva also means Consciousness (caitanya), peace (śāntam), purity (śuci), final beatitude (mokṣa), sacredness (pavitratā) and well-being (kalyāṇam).

Pārvatī symbolizes prakṛti (matter) or māyā (the power of the Lord). When Śiva wields His māyā, He is called Īśvara – the Lord of the universe.

The holy river Ganga emerges from the matted locks of Lord Śiva. Ganga symbolizes knowledge and devotion. The Lord gives the highest place to knowledge and devotion. He is the very source of both. He manages to keep His head cool with the holy and icy waters of Ganga whilst facing all circumstances!

With Mother Ganga on His head and Goddess Pārvatī by His side, Lord Śiva continues to meditate. It signifies, that He has won over passion. Śiva wears the crescent moon on his head. The moon is the deity of the mind. Śiva is one, who has controlled His mind.

Śiva's neck is blue, since He swallowed the poison, that emerged from the churning of the Milky Ocean. Only the brave and mighty can swallow difficulties, and withstand the vicious and poisonous brunt of circumstances without collapsing, or at least without being adversely affected. It becomes their glory. Also, He did not allow His head or heart to get poisoned or embittered. He went through the challenges with admirable fortitude and forbearance and with a smile on His face.

Snakes of all sizes and shapes serve as the ornaments of Śiva. That, which creates fear and revulsion, when it comes in contact with the Lord, becomes His glory.

One with great qualities is welcomed and respected everywhere.[1] The Lord accepts those, who lack virtues, are dull, ignored, rejected and even considered repulsive by the world.[2] So even ghosts, the physically and mentally challenged and snakes find a place with Him.

The Lord smears the ashes from the cremation ground all over His body. He has burnt to ashes the identification with the body in the fire of Self-

---

[1] गणीहि गुणीहि साहिब लहाई – विनय पत्रिका

[2] समीचीन को अधम अगुण आलसी पालिहाई – विनय पत्रिका

knowledge. Also, the final destination of the body is the cremation ground. One should remember always, that the body we pamper so much, will one day be reduced to ashes. We should, therefore, not get too attached to it, accept the changes in it without resistance and learn to age gracefully. All this, the worshipper understands, as he or she meditates on the form of the Lord.

Śiva Mānasa Pūjā

The verses of Śiva Mānasa Pūjā begin with the second step of the ritualistic worship.

रत्नैः कल्पितमासनं हिमजलैः स्नानं च दिव्याम्बरं
नानारत्नविभूषितं मृगमदामोदाङ्कितं चन्दनम् ।
जातीचम्पकबिल्वपत्ररचितं पुष्पं च धूपं तथा
दीपं देव दयानिधे पशुपते हृत्कल्पितं गृह्यताम् ॥१ ॥

ratnaiḥ kalpitam-āsanaṁ himajalaiḥ snānaṁ ca divyāmbaraṁ
nānāratna-vibhūṣitaṁ mṛgamadāmodāṅkitaṁ candanam,
jātī-campaka-bilvapatra-racitaṁ puṣpaṁ ca dhūpaṁ tathā
dīpaṁ deva dayānidhe paśupate hṛtkalpitaṁ gṛhyatām. (1)

1. **रत्नैः कल्पितम् आसनं** – the bejewelled throne; **हिमजलैः स्नानं** – a cool water ritual bath; **च** – and: **नानारत्नविभूषितं दिव्याम्बरं** – divine apparel bedecked with various precious stones; **मृगमदामोदाङ्कितं चन्दनम्** – sandal paste mixed with fragrance of musk; **जातीचम्पकबिल्वपत्ररचितं पुष्पं** – (offering of) flowers like jātī and campaka, and also the bilva leaf; **च** – and; **धूपं**

– incence; दीपं – divine light; तथा – also; देव – O Lord; दयानिधे – O compassionate one; पशुपते – O Lord of all; हृत्कल्पितं – (worship) imagined in my heart; गृह्यताम् – please accept

1. *O compassionate one, the Lord of all, please do accept this worship visualized in my heart as offering of a bejewelled throne, a cool water ritual bath, divine apparel bedecked with various precious stones, sandal paste mixed with the fragrance of musk, fragrant flowers like jātī and campaka and the bilva leaf, incense and the divine light.*

Everything in the world is created by Him and belongs to Him. In our worship we pick out the best of His creation and offer it to Him with love. The beauty and the sanctity of the offerings and the ceremony fulfil our senses and mind.

A bejewelled throne (ratnaiḥ kalpitam-āsanam) – It surely befits the ruler of the world (Īśvara) to be seated in the best imaginable throne. The devotee prays, 'O Lord, I have mentally created a palatial temple for your worship.[1]

[1] तेरे पूजन को भगवान बना मन-मन्दिर आलीशान।

A cool water ritual bath (himajalaiḥ snānam) – Lord Śiva resides on the snowbound Mount Kailash, yet prefers a cool water shower![1] The ceremonial pot of water over the Śiva-liṅga, from which water continuously drips, signifies the continuous flow of thoughts towards the Lord. People spend hours in bathing, dressing and grooming themselves. They spend thousands in clothes, toiletries, perfumes, make-up and jewellery. They find time and money for worshipping the body (deha pūjā), but complain that they do not have time and the means to worship the Lord (deva pūjā)! By worshipping the Lord, our mind shifts from our body to the Lord's form, and thus reduces our attachment and identification with our body.

Divine apparel bedecked with various precious stones (nānā-ratna-vibhūṣitaṁ divyāmbaram) – Lord Śiva usually wears tiger skin signifying dispassion and fearlessness. (Dispassion alone gives fearlessness).[2] However, in our mental worship we offer Him the best materials adorning His divine form in the most beautiful manner.

---

1 अभिषेक प्रियः शिवः (*abhiṣeka priyaḥ śivaḥ*)

2 वैराग्यं एव अभयम् – वैराग्य शतकम्-३१

Sandal paste mixed with the fragrance of musk (mṛgamadāmodāṅkitaṁ candanam) – The tilak or pottu, applied on the forehead and feet of the Lord in the form of a dot, is a mark of respect and for decoration. On the Śiva-liṅga, it is applied as a tripuṇḍra (three parallel horizontal lines with a dot in the centre). Many Hindus too, wear this mark on the forehead as a remembrance of the Lord, as a religious mark or for decoration.

The flowers of jātī and campaka and the bilva leaf (jātī-campaka-bilva-patra-racitaṁ puṣpam) – Lord Śiva has made His worship very easy. You can worship Him even with the dhatūrā flower, which is a wild flower found almost everywhere in India. In a physical worship the best we can offer are seasonal flowers, but in a mental worship we can decorate His form and altar with the most fragrant, exotic and heavenly flowers. Flowers signify everything, which is delicate, soft, beautiful, fragrant, attractive and refreshing. The Lord too, has these qualities.

The bilva leaf grows amidst thorns, yet has great qualities. 'The offering of each bilva leaf, which is three petalled, representing the three qualities (sattva, rajas and tamas), the three-eyed Śiva and the three weapons destroys the sins of three births.'[1]

Incense and showing of divine light (dhūpaṁ ca dīpam) – All our senses are employed in the worship of the Lord. The fragrance of the incense sticks and the smoke wafting from them, the beautiful brass lamps glowing with lights and illumining the divine form of the Lord, all create a divinely blissful experience.

O Paśupati! (paśupate) – paśu – animal, pati – master. Śiva is the Lord of all animals and the Master of all animalistic tendencies. The individual, who gives reality only to the seen or gross, is like an animal[2] (an ignorant and deluded being). Śiva is the Lord of all living beings – the knowledgeable and the ignorant, the divine and the demoniac, the great and the ignoble. Nandī, the vehicle of Śiva symbolizes dharma or righteousness. Śiva is the master of dharma, so one, who lives his life according to dharma, attains Śiva.

---

1 त्रिदलं त्रिगुणाकारं त्रिनेत्रं च त्रियायुधम्।
त्रिजन्मपापसंहारं एकबिल्वं शिवार्पणम्॥ – बिल्वाष्टकम्-१

2 पश्यति इति पशुः (*paśyati iti paśuḥ*)

The worship continues –

सौवर्णे नवरत्नखण्डरचिते पात्रे घृतं पायसं
भक्ष्यं पञ्चविधं पयोदधियुतं रम्भाफलं पानकम् ।
शाकानामयुतं जलं रुचिकरं कर्पूरखण्डोज्ज्वलं
ताम्बूलं मनसा मया विरचितं भक्त्या प्रभो स्वीकुरु ॥२॥

sauvarṇe navaratna-khaṇḍaracite pātre ghṛtaṁ pāyasaṁ
bhakṣyaṁ pañcavidhaṁ payodadhiyutaṁ rambhā-phalaṁ pānakam,
śākānām-ayutaṁ jalaṁ rucikaraṁ karpūra-khaṇḍojjvalaṁ
tāmbūlaṁ manasā mayā viracitaṁ bhaktyā prabho svīkuru. (2)

2. सौवर्णे – in gold; नवरत्नखण्डरचिते – with the nine precious stones embedded in it; पात्रे – vessels; घृतं – (with) clarified butter; पायसं – sweet-dish made of milk; भक्ष्यं – food; पञ्चविधं – of five types; पयोदधियुतं – with milk and curd; रम्भाफलं – banana; पानकम् – sweet juice; शाकानाम् अयुतं – various vegetables; जलं रुचिकरं कर्पूरखण्ड-उज्ज्वलं – fragrant, clear and sweet water with camphor; ताम्बूलं – betel leaf; मनसा – mentally; मया – by me; विरचितं – have created; भक्त्या – with devotion; प्रभो – O Lord; स्वीकुरु – please accept

2. *O Lord! I have with devotion visualized five types of food in gold vessels embedded with nine precious stones, with clarified butter, milk and curds, bananas and sweet juice, various vegetables and fragrant, clear and sweet water with camphor and betel leaf. Please do accept my offering.*

The Lord (Prabhu) – The Lord is all-capable. He has full freedom in action. He can do, undo or do things differently any time, every time.

Gold vessels (sauvarṇe pātre) – Śiva normally carries a mendicant's begging bowl (kamaṇḍalu). The devotee requests the Lord to keep it aside and eat a sumptuous feast in royal style!

Five types of food (bhakṣyaṁ pañcavidham) – There are five ways in which food is eaten. Most foods like rice or wheat is chewed (bhakṣyam), honey or pickle are licked (lehyam), water or soup drunk (peyam), toffees are sucked (coṣyam), pills and powders are swallowed.

I have made all this with devotion (bhaktyā viracitam) – The devotee sings, The Lord considers the relationship of love as the highest one. He ignored the grand feast offered by King Duryodhana and ate simple food at the house of His devotee, Vidura.[1] Food cooked with devotion has a special flavour of love. Śrī Kṛṣṇa fondly recalled and praised the taste of the uncooked pounded rice gifted to Him by His poor childhood friend Kucelā, as it was offered with love.

---

1 सबसे ऊँची प्रेम सगाई। दुर्योधन को मेवा त्याग्यो। साग विदुर घर खाई॥ – सूरदास

After a sumptuous meal (āhāra) it is now time for entertainment (vihāra).

छत्रं चामरयोर्युगं व्यजनकं चादर्शकं निर्मलं
वीणाभेरिमृदङ्गकाहलकला गीतं च नृत्यं तथा ।
साष्टाङ्गं प्रणतिः स्तुतिर्बहुविधा ह्येतत्समस्तं मया
सङ्कल्पेन समर्पितं तव विभो पूजां गृहाण प्रभो ॥३॥

chatraṁ cāmarayor-yugaṁ vyajanakaṁ cādarśakaṁ nirmalaṁ
vīṇā-bheri-mṛdaṅga-kāhalakalā gītaṁ ca nṛtyaṁ tathā,
sāṣṭāṅgaṁ praṇatiḥ stutirbahuvidhā hyetat-samastaṁ mayā
saṅkalpena samarpitaṁ tava vibho pūjāṁ gṛhāṇa prabho. (3)

3. छत्रं – royal umbrella; चामरयोः-युगं – a pair of special royal fans (chowry); व्यजनकं – ornate fan; च – and; आदर्शकं – mirror; निर्मलं – clear; वीणाभेरिमृदङ्गकाहलकला – the music of the vīṇā (a stringed instrument), kettle drum, drum (tabor), a large bass drum; गीतं – song; च – and; नृत्यं – dance; तथा – also; साष्टाङ्गं – with eight limbs; प्रणतिः – prostration; स्तुतिः – the singing of praises; बहुविधा – in many ways; हि-एतत् समस्तं – all this; मया सङ्कल्पेन – with my mind; समर्पितं – offered; तव

– to You; विभो – O all-pervading Lord; पूजां – worship; गृहाण – accept; प्रभो – O Lord

3. *O all-pervading Lord, do accept the royal umbrella, the pair of special royal fans (chowry), ornate fan, a clear mirror, the music of the vīṇā, kettle drum, drum, large bass drum, song, dance, prostrations with eight limbs, and the singing of praises in many ways. All this I offer to You as my mental worship.*

We give our honoured guests a 'red carpet treatment'. The devotee feels that every conceivable royal comfort and form of entertainment must be offered to the King of all kings, the Lord. This entertainment of the Lord is called rājopacāra.

Clear mirror (ādarśakam) – A mirror reflects everything and keeps nothing. It enables us to see ourselves (introspect), remove our flaws (doṣāpanaya), add to our beauty (guṇādhāna) and correct defects (hīnāṅgapūrti). We feel good to see ourselves in a mirror, but get mad if someone else shows us a mirror! Thus, the vain look at themselves endlessly to satisfy their ego, and some to reassure themselves.

Why show a mirror to the Lord? The whole world is His creation reflected in Him in all its glory. The reflected form holds a special beauty. Mount Kailash reflected in the Manasarovar Lake is breathtaking. The Lord has no vanity as all is His reflection alone.

The music of the vīṇā... rhythm, song and dance (vīṇā... kāhalakalā, gītaṁ ca nṛtyam) – Lord Śiva assumed the form of Naṭarāja and played the ḍamaru. From it emerged all the fine arts – music, dance, literature and so on. Temples have always patronized all the arts, since in their pure form, they are means to reach Him. Some artists find fulfilment in offering their art to Him. Great artists say that their finest compositions and masterpieces have been inspired by Him. In traditional worship as we offer rājopacāra, the priests chant—

O lover of instrumental music, song, mantras of the *Ṛg-veda,* do accept this music, song, *Ṛg-veda* mantras...[1]

---

[1] वाद्य प्रिय वाद्यं अवधारय।
गान प्रिय गानं अवधारय।
ऋग्वेद प्रिय ऋग्वेदं अवधारय।....

Prostrations with eight limbs of the body touching the floor (sāṣṭāṅgaṁ praṇatiḥ) – Prostrations are a way of respecting and acknowledging the greatness of another. Sāṣṭāṅga praṇāma is done by prostrating fully with the feet, knees, chest, forehead and arms touching the ground. The most important is the forehead signifying the surrender of the ego at His altar.

Singing praise in many ways (bahuvidhā stutiḥ) – There is always an element of exaggeration in worldly praise. It is quite the opposite when we praise the Lord, as any amount of praise falls miserably short of His glories! The Lord has infinite qualities in infinite measure. How can we adequately praise Him? In attempting to praise Him, we realize our own limitations, our deepest feelings get kindled and our mind gets purified. The Lord does not ask for or need our praise. However, like a child saying that he has the best mother in the world, the Lord is pleased with our attempts at His praise.

The all-pervading Lord (vibho) – Becoming all, the Lord is all-pervading.[1]

---

[1] विविधं भवति (*vividhaṁ bhavati*)

What is the culmination of all ritualistic worship?

आत्मा त्वं गिरिजा मतिः सहचराः प्राणाः शरीरं गृहं
पूजा ते विषयोपभोगरचना निद्रा समाधिस्थितिः ।
सञ्चारः पदयोः प्रदक्षिणविधिः स्तोत्राणि सर्वा गिरो
यद्यत्कर्म करोमि तत्तदखिलं शम्भो तवाराधनम् ॥४ ॥

ātmā tvaṁ girijā matiḥ sahacarāḥ prāṇāḥ śarīraṁ gṛhaṁ
pūjā te viṣayopabhoga-racanā nidrā samādhi-sthitiḥ,
sañcāraḥ padayoḥ pradakṣiṇavidhiḥ stotrāṇi sarvā giro
yadyatkarma karomi tattad-akhilaṁ śambho
tavārādhanam. (4)

4. आत्मा – the Self; त्वं – Thou art; गिरिजा – Girijā; मतिः – the intellect; सहचराः – companions; प्राणाः – the vital airs; शरीरं – body; गृहं – abode; पूजा – worship; ते – Thy; विषयोपभोगरचना – the enjoyment of objects; निद्रा – sleep; समाधिस्थितिः – the state of absorption in meditation; सञ्चारः – moving around; पदयोः – with the feet; प्रदक्षिणविधिः – circumambulation; स्तोत्राणि – praises; सर्वा – all; गिरो – speech; यत् यत् – whatever; कर्म – action; करोमि – I do; तत् तत् – that; अखिलं – all; शम्भो – O Śambhu; तव – Your; आराधनम् – worship

4. *Thou art my Self, my intellect is Thy consort Girijā, my vital airs are Thy companions, my body is Thy abode, my enjoyment of objects is Thy worship, my sleep is the state of absorption in meditation, all my moving around is Thy circumambulation and all my words are Thy praises. O Śambhu! Whatever actions I do is Thy worship alone.*

When we start the ritualistic worship we initially focus on the materials, method and action. Then the attention shifts to the attitude or feeling behind the action. What starts as a mechanical routine, later becomes an expression of love. The worship which starts outside, matures to become worship within and culminates in serving the world with a worshipful attitude.

Thou art the Self (ātmā tvam) – The idol we worship represents the omnipotent, omniscient and omnipresent Lord. Being everywhere the Lord also resides within us. He is the life-giver and the very life in us. He is self-evident Consciousness within that enlivens all, the Existence within that sustains all, the Bliss within that gives joy to all. He is the very Self that expresses as 'I' in all our experiences, the centre of our world and existence.[1] Saint Tulasīdāsa says, 'Knowing the whole world to be Sītā-Rāma (the Lord), I prostrate to all with folded hands.'

1 सर्वस्य चाहं हृदि सन्निविष्टः – गीता-१५·१५

Such Knowledge results in serving the world with the attitude of worshipping the Lord.[1]

A devotee went each day to the temple and prayed. One day it struck him, 'Each day I keep talking to God through my prayers. Never have I listened to Him. Today let me hear what He has to say'. So he was silent, but his mind kept chattering. He thought, 'I still cannot hear Him, so let me silence my mind. When he quietened his mind, he went into a state of deep meditation. He, thereafter, never visited the temple. When asked, he said, "I have realized the Lord within. Now, it makes no difference if I worship him within or without." However, we should note that this is only for the highest type of devotee. Till we reach those heights of devotion, temple visits and the like are important means in fostering devotion.

My intellect is Thy consort Girijā (girijā matiḥ) – Sati, the daughter of Dakṣa burnt herself in the yogic fire, to be born again as Girijā, the daughter of Himavān. She performed severe austerities to attain Śiva as her husband. Girijā thus represents an unshakeable intellect, determined to attain the Lord. Girijā is māyā who has the three qualities of

1 जगतः ईशाधीयुक्तसेवनं
अष्टमूर्तिभृत् देवपूजनम् – उपदेश सार-५

sattva, rajas and tamas. The intellect too, is sāttvika, rājasika and tāmasika. Māyā controls and deludes man, but the same māyā is controlled by the Lord (Māyāpati). He wields His māyā to create the world. The intellect deludes the ignorant but for a wise person, it is instrumental in him achieving greatness and noble deeds. It is the intellect that guides man[1] and helps discriminate between right and wrong.

The five vital airs are His companions (sahacarā prāṇāḥ) – Prāṇa, apāna, vyāna, udāna and samāna are the five physiological functions of breathing, evacuation, circulation, reversal (like sneezing) and digestion, so very vital for life and all activities. They are the indicators of life in the body and accompany the individual when life ebbs out. Lord Śiva manifests as life in us, hence the vital airs are like the Śiva-gaṇas, His companions, vitalizing all activities.

The body is His abode (śarīraṁ gṛham) – Saint Tukārāma says, 'This body is the temple for the Lord, the Self within.[2]

Sense enjoyment is Your worship (pūjā te viṣaya-upabhoga-racanā) – The wise man knows that all

---

1 बुद्धिं तु सारथिं विद्धि .... – कठोपनिषद्-१·३·३

2 देह देवाचे मन्दिर, आत आत्मा परमेश्वर – संत तुकाराम

pleasures (viṣayānanda) are but a reflection of the infinite Bliss of the Self (Brahmānanda). Hence, every sense perception becomes a worship of the Lord or the Self alone. For one who comprehends this, no special time is required for worship. All of life is a worship. Sipping a hot cup of coffee, Pūjya Gurudev remarked, 'Who says coffee does not have Brahmānanda?'

My sleep is a state of meditation (nidrā samādhi sthitiḥ) – The mature devotee knows that the Lord is one without a second. Nothing other than Him truly exists. Wherever his mind goes, the devotee experiences the Lord or the Truth alone.[1] The state of revelling in the Truth is called 'absorption in meditation.' He experiences open-eyed meditation in every waking experience and close-eyed meditation in sleep. This effortless state of being is called 'sahaja samādhi'. We sleep even whilst attempting meditation, while the wise meditate even as they sleep!

Moving around is Thy circumambulation (sañcāra pradakśiṇā-vidhi) – Circumambulation signifies keeping God as the centre of our lives, as we move around in the world. Also, during pradakṣiṇā we keep Him on our right. This implies that we must always walk the path of righteousness. Knowing

1 यत्र यत्र मनो याति तत्र तत्र समाधयः – वाक्य सुधा-३०

that He is everywhere, all movement becomes as sacred and circumambulation of the Lord.

All words are Thy praises (stotrāṇi sarvā giro) – That which cannot be described, but that because of which we speak, is the Self or God.[1] The Lord appeared before young Prahlāda. He was so overwhelmed with devotion that he could not speak. He remained silent staring at the Lord. The Lord touched His conch to his cheek and that divine touch inspired Prahlāda to sing beautiful words in praise of the Lord.[2]

One should not worry if one does not know Sanskrit. The Lord can be praised in any language. Just as the mother is pleased by the prattling of her child, every word of a true devotee pleases the Lord. Sweet words of love delight our heart. The Lord within is delighted by our words of love.

With such knowledge of oneness whatever I do is His worship alone (yat yat karma karomi tat tat akhilaṁ śambho tavārādhanam).

---

1 यद्वाचानभ्युदितं येन वागभ्युद्यते तदेव ब्रह्म··· – केनोपनिषद् – १·१·४

2 योऽन्त प्रविश्य मम वाचमिमां प्रसुप्तां
सञ्जीवयत्यखिलशक्तिधरः स्वधाम्ना।
अन्यांश्चहस्तचरणश्रवणत्वगादीन्
प्राणान्नमो भगवते पुरुषाय तुभ्यम्॥ – श्रीमद् भागवत-४·९·६

We end the mental worship with –

करचरणकृतं वाक्कायजं कर्मजं वा
श्रवणनयनजं वा मानसं वापराधम् ।
विहितमविहितं वा सर्वमेतत्क्षमस्व
जय जय करुणाब्धे श्री महादेव शम्भो ॥५॥

kara-caraṇa-kṛtaṁ vāk-kāyajaṁ karmajaṁ vā
śravaṇa-nayanajaṁ vā mānasaṁ vāparādham,
vihitam-avihitaṁ vā sarvametat-kṣamasva
jaya jaya karuṇābdhe śrī mahādeva śambho. (5)

5. **करचरणकृतं** – done with hand(s) and leg(s); **वाक् कायजं** – born of speech and the body; **कर्मजं** – born of actions; **वा** – or; **श्रवणनयनजं** – born of ear(s) and eye(s); **वा** – or; **मानसं** – (born of) the mind; **वा** – or; **अपराधम्** – errors (sins); **विहितम्** – ordained; **अविहितं** – prohibited; **वा** – or; **सर्वम्** – all; **एतत्** – this; **क्षमस्व** – do forgive; **जय जय** – victory to Thee; **करुणाब्धे** – O compassionate one; **श्री महादेव** – O Mahādeva; **शम्भो** – O Śambhu

5. *O compassionate Mahādeva! O Śambhu! Victory to Thee! Please do forgive all the errors committed (by us)*

with the hands, legs, speech, body, through actions, the ears, eyes, mind or by (not doing) ordained actions or (by doing) prohibited actions.

In Indian culture there is a beautiful saying, 'Please forgive any shortcomings in hosting you'.[1] We say this to a guest before bidding him farewell. To err is human, to forgive divine. We tend to err and commit mistakes knowingly or unknowingly ever so often. We should be alert enough to realize our mistakes, regret doing the same (paścāttāpa), seek forgiveness (kṣamā yācanā), resolve never to repeat them, and do our best to compensate for the same by expiatory action (prāyaścitta).

The devotee having performed the worship prays, 'Since I do not know fully how to welcome You, bid You farewell or worship You (as per scriptural injunctions), I must have erred. O Lord, so please do forgive me'.[2]

'O Lord, may all that I have done, please You, even though there may have been mistakes in the chanting

---

1 भूल-चूक माफ करना (*bhūla-cūka māpha karanā*)

2 आवाहनं न जानामि न जानामि विसर्जनम्।
पूजां चैव न जानामि क्षमस्व परमेश्वर॥

of the mantras and the performance of rituals, I may have fallen short in strength and faith, and I may have erred in selecting the auspicious time in following the prescribed rules and in the proper offering of the appropriate kinds of food'.[1]

In fact 'I commit thousands of mistakes each day and night. O Lord, consider me Thy servant and forgive me.'[2]

How does man commit mistakes and sins?

Mistakes or sins committed with our limbs (kara caraṇa kṛtam) – Hands do wrong when they serve the selfish, faithless and criminals, steal, aggrandize and hurt others, and do not worship God or serve His devotees or give in charity. To go where we should not (places of vices and seeking the company of the unholy) and not to go where we should (satsaṅga – sacred places and holy company) is to sin with the legs.

---

1 मन्त्र-लोपे तन्त्र-लोपे क्रिया-लोपे शक्ति-लोपे श्रद्धा-लोपे काल-लोपे नियम-लोपे नैवेद्यादि विहित-लोपे च भगवत् प्रीतिकरं भूयात् इति।

2 अपराध सहस्राणि क्रियन्तेऽहर्निशं मया।
दासोऽयमिति मां मत्वा क्षमस्व परमेश्वर॥

Mistakes or sins born of speech, body and actions (vāk-kāyajaṁ-karmajam) – The speech does wrong when we criticize others or gossip, utter untruths and harsh words and not sing His glories. To worship only the body (deha pūjā) and not the Lord (deva pūjā), to do evil actions and not to work for self-improvement is to sin through the body and by our actions.

Mistakes and sins born of ears and eyes (śravaṇa-nayanajam) – We do wrong through our ears, when we listen to gossip, when we ignore good advice, and do not listen to the glories of God. To see and appreciate only the inauspicious and not His glories is to sin with the eyes.

(Born of) the mind (mānasam) – To think evil, plot devious acts, and never meditate on God or enquire about the Truth is to sin mentally.

Ordained or prohibited (vihitaṁ-avihitam) – We do wrong when we partially follow the ordained or do what is prohibited.

Here, the devotee asks for a blanket forgiveness covering all his sins and mistakes. Such forgiveness

3 *yo yo yāṁ yāṁ tanuṁ bhaktaḥ śraddhayārcitum-icchati,*
tasya tasyācalāṁ śraddhāṁ tāmeva vidadhāmyaham
– *Gītā*-7.21 14

1 *yasyāṅke ca vibhāti bhūdharasutā devāpagā mastake*
bhāle bālavidhurgale ca garalaṁ yasyorasi vyālarāṭ,
so'yaṁ bhūtivibhūṣaṇaḥ suravaraḥ sarvārdhipaḥ sarvadā
śarvaḥ sarvagataḥ śivaḥ śaśinibhaḥ śrīśaṅkaraḥ pātu mām.
– *Ayodhyā-kāṇḍa – maṅgalācaraṇa*.......................................15

1 *gaṇīhi guṇīhi sāhiba lahāī.* – *Vinaya Patrikā*........................17

2 *samīcīna ko adhama aguṇa ālasī pālihāī.* – *Vinaya Patrikā*....17

1 *tere pūjana ko bhagavāna banā mana-mandira ālīśāna.* 20

2 *vairāgyaṁ eva abhayam.* – *Vairāgya Śatakam*-31 21

1 *tridalaṁ triguṇākāraṁ trinetraṁ ca triyāyudham,*
trijanmapāpasaṁhāraṁ eka-bilvaṁ śivārpaṇam.
– *Bilvāṣṭakam*-1..23

1 *sabase ūm̐cī prema sagāī, duryodhana ko mevā tyāgyo,*
sāga vidura ghara khāī....' – *Sūradāsa* 26

1 *vādya priya vādyaṁ avadhāraya,*
gāna priya gānaṁ avadhāraya,
ṛgveda priya ṛgvedaṁ avadhāraya.... 29

1 *sarvasya cāhaṁ hṛdi sanniviṣṭaḥ* – *Gītā*-15.15......................32

1 *jagataḥ īśadhī-yukta-sevanaṁ,*
aṣṭa-mūrti-bhṛt devapūjanam. – *Upadeśa Sāra*-5..................33

1 *buddhiṁ tu sārathiṁ viddhi* – *Kaṭhopaniṣad*-1.3.3..................34